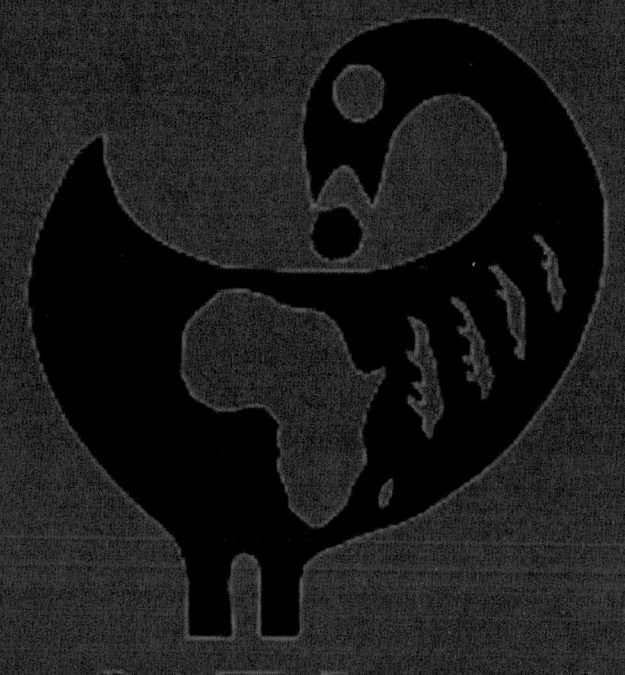

Sankofa Educational Service

Hardcover ISBN:979-8333240279
Paperback ISBN: 979-8332893520
Published By Book Writer Corner
Sankofa Educational Services
©2024 Letta S. Baker Mason
All rights reserved. No part of the book may be reproduced, stored in a retrieval system, or transmitted in any form or by any means, electronic, mechanical, photocopying, recording, or otherwise, without prior permission of the publisher.
sankofaeducationalservices.com

This Book Belongs To

_____

Dear Families, Scholars, and Educators,

Sankofa, Sankofa is more than a children's book—it is a powerful family and community tool designed to uplift and celebrate the diversity of ethnic groups, languages, and cultural traditions. This book is filled with joyful activities suitable for any learning and cultural environment.

The artwork in Sankofa, Sankofa is truly mesmerizing and is created with scholars in mind, from preschool through high school and beyond. Let the pages captivate you and fill your heart with the love of self and others.

Integration into Homes, Schools, and Communities

Homes:
Encourage family reading sessions where parents and children can explore the stories and activities together.

Use the book as a guide to celebrate cultural holidays and traditions, creating a deeper understanding and appreciation within the family.

Engage in art and craft projects inspired by the book's illustrations and themes, fostering creativity and bonding.

Schools:
Incorporate the book into various subjects such as language arts, social studies, and art. Tailored lesson plans are available for different grade levels.

Host workshops and discussions around the themes of diversity, inclusion, and cultural heritage, using the book as a central resource.

Utilize the book in literacy programs to enhance reading, writing, and comprehension skills through engaging content.

Community:
Partner with local libraries to host read-aloud sessions, cultural events, and art exhibitions featuring the book.

Organize community events that celebrate cultural diversity, using the book as a focal point for activities and discussions.

Feature the book in local cultural festivals, allowing families and community members to participate in themed activities and learn together.

We are thrilled to offer curriculum materials from preschool through high school, tailored to different skill levels. These resources aim to increase literacy, mathematical understanding, and writing proficiency across content areas.

To request the curriculum or for more information, please email us at sankofaedu2003@gmail.com.

Thank you for your support and dedication to fostering a love of learning and celebrating diversity within our community.

Warm regards,
Letta S. Baker Mason, MA, M.Ed.

Sankofa, Sankofa

Author Letta S. Baker Mason
Illustrator Mark Fraley
Publisher Book Writer Corner
sankofaeducationalservices.com

Dedication

I dedicate this book to all the Scholars of
the African Diaspora.
Special dedication to my grandbabies,
Ramadan, Minaya, Raylynn, DolRay Jr., India, Eshaan,
Loyal, Maliyah, Raelle, Lil Addis,
Lamonta Jr., and Ky'Lea Imani
My greatnieces and nephews.
To my beautiful husband with the biggest smile, David Van
Mason, who has become an ancestor.

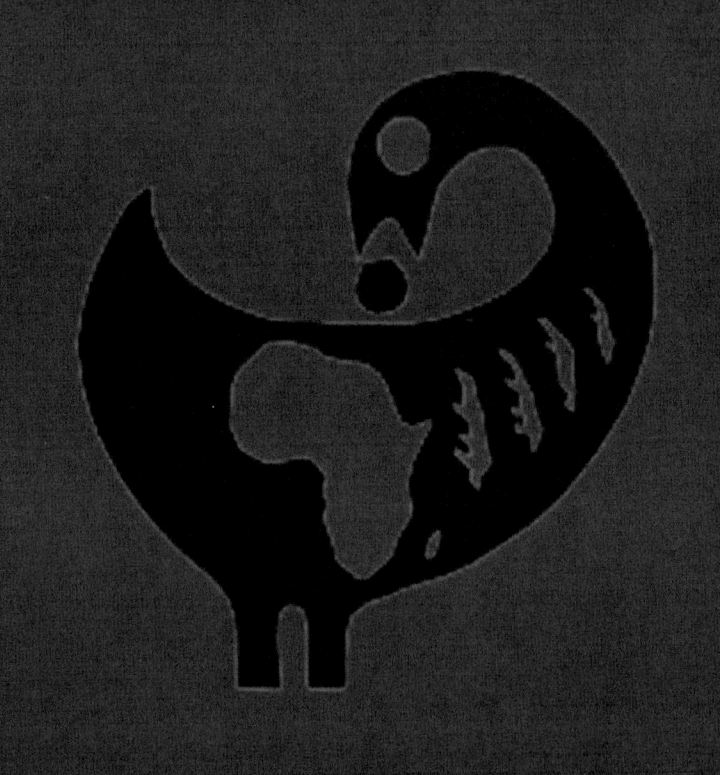

The art medium used in Sankofa is diverse and is meant to engage Scholars in their craft using various mediums to express their creativity and understanding of Sankofa. Through the concept of Sankofa, individuals will explore and reconnect with their culture and family history, often using artistic expression as a medium for this journey. Sankofa, a word from the Akan language of Ghana, means "to go back and fetch," symbolizing the importance of remembering and learning from the past to build a better future.

Art plays a crucial role in this process. By using different forms of art mediums—such as painting, collaging, music, dance, photographs, sketching, and digital media—Scholars can delve into their heritage and bring forth stories, traditions, and experiences that resonate with their cultural identity. This creative process allows for personal exploration and invites Scholars and audiences to engage with and learn from these rich cultural narratives.

In Sankofa, art becomes a bridge between past and present, enabling a deeper understanding of one's roots and fostering a connection to one's ancestry. Through this artistic journey, the past is honored, and its lessons are carried forward, enriching both individual lives and the collective cultural consciousness.

Also By Letta S. Baker Mason

Connecting Students of African Descent with a Global Perspective on the Intra-African Connection Through Literacy ©2002

Bringing The Arts to Life: Using the Multiple Intelligences and Culturally Relevant Materials"
Workbook (Spanish/English version)©2003

Bringing the Arts to Life: Using the Multiple Intelligences and Culturally Responsive Curriculum:
S.T.E.A.M.S Edition (Text 1 Harriet Tubman and Text 2, George Washington Carver) ©2023

Bringing the Arts To Life: Using the Multiple Intelligences and Culturally Responsive Curriculum Math Edition ©2024

Afro-Futuristic Adventures with Granville T. Woods: The Figure 8 Rollercoaster ©2024

Sankofa, Sankofa, Sankofa!

San Ko Fa
1 1 1

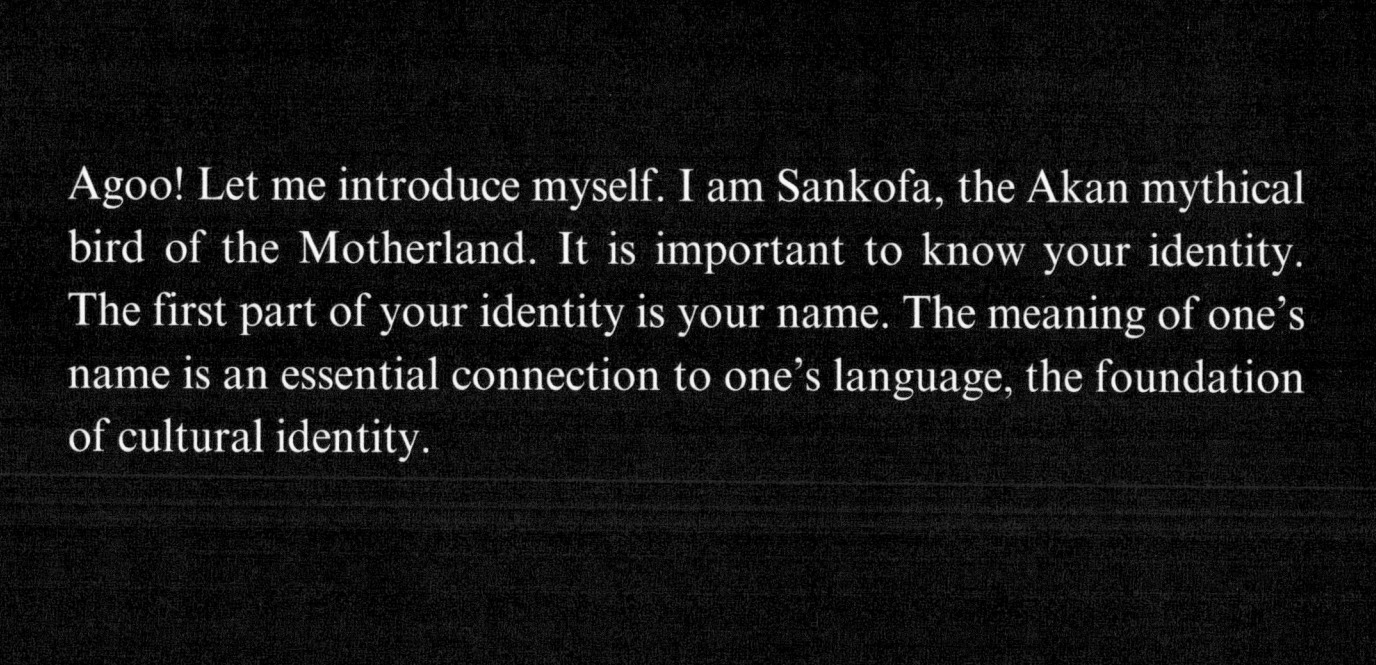

Agoo! Let me introduce myself. I am Sankofa, the Akan mythical bird of the Motherland. It is important to know your identity. The first part of your identity is your name. The meaning of one's name is an essential connection to one's language, the foundation of cultural identity.

Activity: In what ways can you find the meaning of your name?

ASANTE TWI

Let's pronounce this together A San Te Tree!

We can find the meaning of our name by asking our family members or looking it up in books or online.

Sometimes our names have special stories or come from different languages, and learning about them can help us understand our heritage and culture better.

Sankofa, Sankofa, Sankofa!

San Ko Fa
1   1   1

In Hausa, a language spoken in parts of West Africa, "tar" might be related to the word "tarayya," which means "society" or "community."

In Kiswahili, "isha" means "life" or "alive."

In Kiswahili, "Mila" means "customs" or "traditions."

In Amharic, "La" can mean "for" or "to."

In Kiswahili, "si" is a negation word meaning "no" or "not."

Sankofa, Sankofa, Sankofa!

San Ko Fa
1   1   1

Breaking down the spelling of our names involves examining each letter and considering its significance. By doing this, we can uncover any hidden meanings or connections to our identity. For example, each letter in a name may represent a characteristic, a cultural symbol, or a family tradition.

This process allows us to understand the deeper significance of our names and how they contribute to our sense of self and cultural identity.

SARAH'

Let's take the name "Sarah'" as an example. When we break down the spelling of "Sarah," we see that "rah" is a part of the name. In some cultures, "rah" or "ra" is associated with the sun. Therefore, someone named "Sarah" might interpret their name as having a connection to the sun or light, which could symbolize warmth, brightness, or energy. This example illustrates how breaking down the spelling of our names can reveal meaningful associations and connections to our cultural identity.

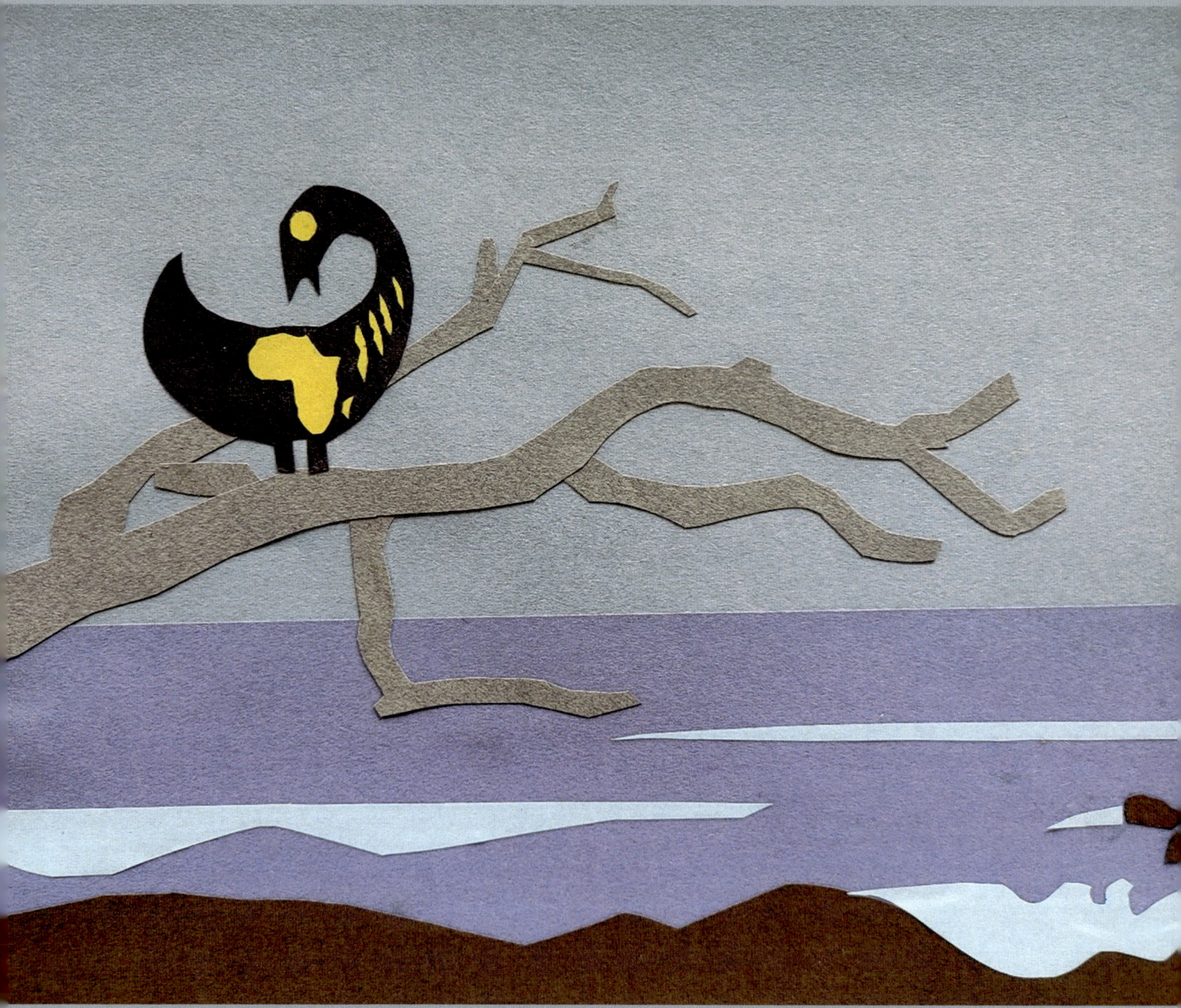

Sankofa is a word in the Twi language of Ghana. The name Sankofa means, "Go Back and Fetch What you Have Lost" In Akan Language it is pronounced "se wo were fi na wosan kofa a yenki." Which mean It's not too late to fetch what was lost.

Red is for the blood of Black People.

Black is for the beauty of the People.

Green is for the land Stolen from Black People.

The origin of a name can provide insight into its meaning and cultural significance. For example, if your name has African origins, it might have a meaning rooted in African languages or traditions.

Similarly, names from other cultures or regions may have different origins and meanings based on the languages and customs of those areas. Exploring the origin of your name can help you understand its cultural heritage and significance.

Activity: What is the origin of your name?

AFRICA

ACCRA

GHANA

The origin of the name "Sankofa" can be traced back to the Akan people of Ghana, West Africa. In the Akan language, "san" means "return," and "ko" means "go," while "fa" means "take."

Therefore, "Sankofa" can be translated to mean "go back and fetch" or "reach back and get it." The name symbolizes the importance of learning from the past in order to move forward.

Map 34 **WEST-CENTRAL AFRICA**

The Middle Passage was a long and difficult journey across the Atlantic Ocean from Africa to the Americas that enslaved Africans were forced to endure. Picture a vast ocean stretching out as far as the eye can see, with waves crashing against the sides of a big wooden ship. The ship is crowded with people, so packed together that there's hardly any room to move. It's hot and stuffy below the deck, and the air smells salty and musty.

Activity: Ask family members about their migration to America

Now imagine the sound of the waves rocking the ship back and forth, making some people seasick. Others are crying, missing their families and the homes they left behind. There's a feeling of fear and uncertainty in the air as the ship sails farther and farther away from Africa.

Sankofa, Sankofa, Sankofa!

Activity: Have scholars clap to the syllables of
San Ko Fa
 1   1   1

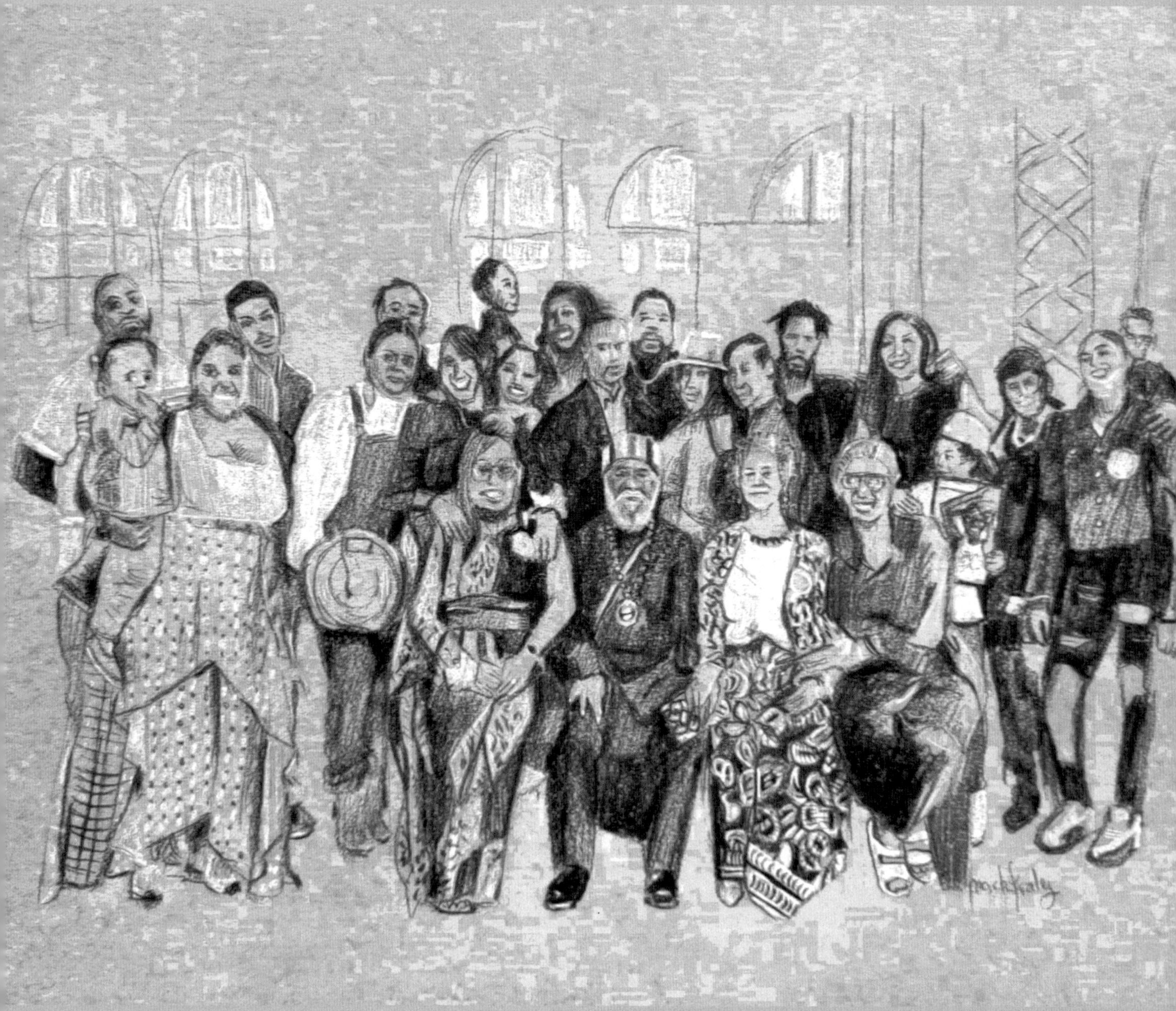

Family and community are extremely important to Sankofa because they provide a sense of belonging, support, and connection to one's roots and identity. In African culture, Family extends beyond just blood relatives to include the larger community, which acts as a source of strength and unity. Sankofa recognizes the significance of family and community in preserving traditions, passing down knowledge, and providing mutual aid and protection. By embracing and celebrating the values of family and community, Sankofa honors the rich cultural heritage and ancestral wisdom that shapes its identity.

Activity: Draw the people who are special to you in your community and share with the learning community. Share names of your community members and their relations.

Mancala

Activity: What are some preferred games you enjoy playing, and what is their origin?

Sankofa's message of "Go back and fetch what we have lost" emphasizes the importance of reclaiming and preserving elements of African heritage that may have been lost or forgotten over time. One such example is the game of mancala, which originated in Africa and holds deep cultural significance. In ancient times, Scholars would play mancala by digging holes in the earth and using pebbles as game pieces.

Despite its humble beginnings, mancala has evolved into a popular game enjoyed by people all around the world. Sankofa reminds us of the value of reconnecting with our cultural roots and rediscovering the traditions that bring us joy and connection.

Dinkinesh, Dinkinesh, Dinkinesh. "Thou Art Beautiful"

"Dinkinesh," also known as "Lucy," is the name given to the fossilized remains of a female hominid discovered in Ethiopia in 1974. These ancient bones belong to a species called Australopithecus afarensis, which lived approximately 3.2 million years ago. The name "Dinkinesh" means "thou art beautiful" in Amharic, one of the languages spoken in Ethiopia.

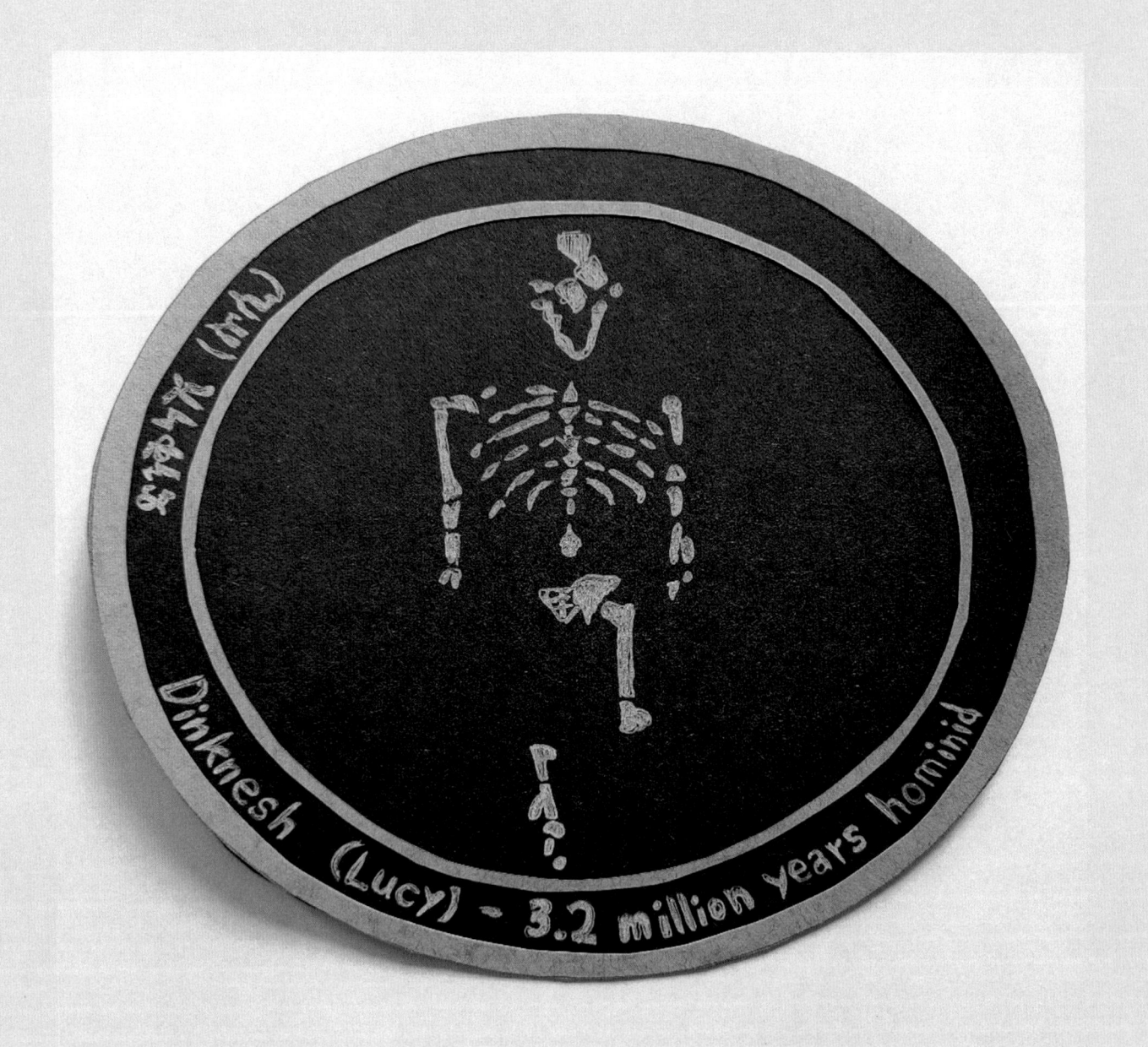

Clap Your Hands!
Din ki nesh
1 1 1

Clap Your Hands!

Din ki nesh

1 1 1

Clap Your Hands!

Din ki nesh

1 1 1

Clap Your Hands!

Din ki nesh

1 1 1

Activity: Instruct scholars to create a visual representation of their family lineage.

Sankofa teaches us that our roots are planted in the African soil that fertilizes our family and community connectedness, from which love blossoms!

Sankofa, Sankofa, Sankofa!

Activity: Have scholars clap to the syllables of
San Ko Fa
1   1   1

We Are Going Back To Get What Is Ours.

Music   Warriors   Food   Agriculture

Activity: Encourage scholars to discuss their favorite music and foods.

Mangos

Cucumber, Peppers, & Cauliflower

Tomatoes

Sweet Potatoes

46

Sankofa guides us through the busy marketplace, where traditional foods serve as a link to various aspects of life. These foods symbolize the importance of sustainable agriculture, teaching us to harvest only what is necessary from the earth without causing harm. For instance, the juicy taste of watermelon not only delights our taste buds but also provides essential nutrients for our health. Similarly, the succulent mango embodies the richness of the land and the abundance it offers.

Djembe Drum

In addition to food, Sankofa highlights the significance of the African Djembe drum. The Djembe drum is a vital form of technology and communication. For example, the rhythmic beats of the drum convey messages across long distances in traditional African societies. Whether warning of impending danger or celebrating community events, the drum plays a central role in fostering unity and cohesion.

Civil Rights Activist
Baba Rev. Kwame John Porter

Sankofa says, "Give reverence to the Elders." In many cultures, elders serve as griots and community historians who pass down knowledge and traditions through oral narratives. They are revered for their wisdom and experience, and their role is to preserve the history, culture, and values of their community by sharing stories, lessons, and insights with younger generations. Griots play a vital role in keeping traditions alive and ensuring that important cultural heritage is passed down from one generation to the next.

Activity: How many different shapes are in the illustration. Can you name the shapes?

Sankofa is a reminder that the future generations are to stand on the shoulders of the ancestors which means to acknowledge and honor the sacrifices and struggles of those who came before us. It signifies recognizing the resilience, wisdom, and contributions of our predecessors, who endured hardships so that future generations could thrive. By standing on their shoulders, we carry forward their legacy, making them proud by continuing their fight for justice, equality, and prosperity. It is a profound acknowledgment of our indebtedness to those who paved the way for our existence and a commitment to honoring their memory through our actions and achievements.

Fly High, Fly High, Fly High!

Activity: Have the Scholars extend their arms outward and raise them upwards while singing "Fly High" to mimic the action of birds flying.

Furthermore, warriors are presented as guardians who protect the community from harm. They embody strength, courage, and resilience, standing ready to defend their people against any threats or challenges they may face. Through their bravery and sacrifice, warriors uphold the values of the community and ensure the safety and well-being of all.

Asè

Civil Rights Activist
Rev. Chester L. Baker

"Asè" is a Yoruba word that is commonly used in African spiritual traditions. It is often translated as "so be it" or "it shall be done." It carries the idea of affirmation and acknowledgment of the power of words or intentions to manifest in reality. In cultural and spiritual contexts, "Asè" is often spoken at the end of prayers, rituals, or declarations, signifying the belief that the desired outcome will come to fruition.

Sankofa, Sankofa, Sankofa!

Activity: Have scholars clap to the syllables of
San Ko Fa
1   1   1

Discussion Questions ??????

→

Discussion Questions

- Which languages can you speak?
- Can you tell me why your name is special?
- What symbols in your home represent your culture?
- Do you know where your ancestors from three generations ago were from?
- Why do we say family and community is important?
- Who is the figure Sankofa?
- Can you describe what Sankofa looks like? Why do people consider Sankofa to be significant?
- What lessons does Sankofa offer us?
- In what ways does Sankofa help us understand our family history?
- Are there any games Sankofa has shown us that come from Africa?
- Why should we pay attention to the tales Sankofa tells?
- If you had to guess, what would you say is Sankofa's favorite meal?
- How might we follow in Sankofa's footsteps to learn from our past?
- What is the meaning behind Sankofa's name?

Skills To Master From Sankofa, Sankofa

→

Speaking and listening
(language development)

- Know and use several hundred words in your home language.
- Use new words on your own.
- Use words to describe actions (such as "running fast") and emotions (such as happy, sad, tired, and scared).
- Talk in sentences of five or six words.
- Listen to others and respond in a group discussion for a short
- Talk in sentences of five or six words.
- Listen to others and respond in a group discussion for a short period. Remember what was said and gain information through listening.
- State your own point of view and likes and dislikes using words, gestures, and/or pictures.
- Join in and makeup songs, chants, rhymes, and games that play with the sounds of language (such as clapping out the rhythm).
- Sing a song or say a poem from memory.

Social Studies →

Social Studies

- Describe family members and understand simple relationships (such as, "Marika is my sister.")
- Adopt the roles of different family members during dramatic play.
- Plan what each role does and then enact it.
- Draw own family, as the child understands it.
- Ask questions about similarities and differences in other people (such as language, hairstyle, and clothing).

Reading →

Reading

- Tell you what is going to happen next in a story. Make up an ending.
- Identify a variety of printed materials (such as books, newspapers, magazines, and cereal boxes).
- Use actions to show ideas from stories, signs, pictures, etc.
- Retell more complicated, familiar stories from memory.

Writing →

Writing

- Make marks, scribbles, or letter-like shapes and identify them as words. Use pretend writing activities during play.
- Use letter-like symbols to make lists, letters, and stories or to label pictures.
- Attempt to copy one or more letters of the alphabet.
- Begin to print or copy own name, and identify at least some of the letters.
- Explore writing letters in different languages.

The Story Behind Sankofa, Sankofa

⟶

The Story Behind Sankofa, Sankofa Sankofa began as a heartfelt poem I wrote after losing my husband, David Van Mason, to prostate cancer. One night, in the middle of overwhelming grief, I woke up and poured my emotions onto the page. I read the poem several times with tears streaming down my cheeks. Despite the sorrow, a profound sense of peace and excitement washed over me, bringing a smile to my face.

The next day, I reached out to Grammy Award Winners Josephine Howell and Medearis MD Dixson, my husband's favorite musician and vocalist. I asked if they could turn the heartfelt poem dedicated to David into a song. Without hesitation, they agreed, and we scheduled a recording session for the following Friday. Interestingly, I was asked to leave the recording session, which could be a story for another best-seller!

When I finally heard the angelic voice and the beautiful music arrangement, I was deeply moved. At that moment, I knew I had to transform the poem into a children's book. I wanted illustrations to bring the words to life, so I contacted Mark Fraley, a colleague whose artwork powerfully demonstrates social justice and equality.

You cannot construct a Sankofa story without the wisdom of elders. I immediately called my father, Rev. Chester L. Baker, who introduced me to the concept of Sankofa. Over thirty years ago, he gifted me a Sankofa statue. My parents have always embodied the meaning of Sankofa through storytelling, music, art, literature, and travel.

In the summer of 2023, my father and I were blessed to embark on our Sankofa journey to Kumasi and Accra, Ghana. Experiencing Ghana with my father was an indescribable honor and joy. The Sankofa team symbolizes identity and diversity, and through this song and book, we hope to share this rich heritage with the world.

Ancestral

Written By Letta S. Baker Mason
Vocals, Josephine Howell
Music Arrangement, Medearis MD Dixson

Fly High, Fly High

Sankofa, Sankofa, Sankofa
Sankofa, Sankofa, Sankofa
Sankofa, Sankofa, Sankofa
Sankofa, Sankofa, Sankofa

Go back!
Go back and fetch what we have lost
Dinkinesh, Dinkinesh, Dinkinesh
Thou art beautiful!

Take me back to the motherland.
Where our roots are planted

Sankofa, Sankofa, Sankofa
Sankofa, Sankofa, Sankofa
Sankofa. Sankofa, Sankofa
Sankofa, Sankofa, Sankofa

We are going back to get what's ours
We are going back to get what's ours

Standing, standing on the shoulders of our Ancestors

Fly High…….. Fly High……………….
Ase'…. Ase'……..
Go back!
Go back and fetch what we have lost

Sankofa, Sankofa, Sankofa
Sankofa, Sankofa, Sankofa
Sankofa. Sankofa, Sankofa
Sankofa, Sankofa, Sankofa

Dinkinesh, Dinkinesh, Dinkinesh
Thou art beautiful!
Take me back to the motherland!
Where our roots are planted

Sankofa, Sankofa, Sankofa
Sankofa, Sankofa, Sankofa
Ase'
Sankofa, Sankofa, Sankofa
Ase'
Sankofa, Sankofa, Sankofa
Ase' Ase'

Meet The Illustrator

→

About the Illustrator

Mark. E. Fraley is an artist and educator who currently lives with his family of 5 in Caldwell, Idaho. He grew up overseas in France and has always looked to portray the wide variety of people and places he has encountered. His book "The Creation of Calm: A Sketchbook Story" details through illustrations and short entries a challenging phase of his life when, in 2008 and 2010, he battled cancer. He has taught as an early childhood special education for over 20 years in Kansas, Washington, Colorado, Albania, and Idaho. His multiple interests converge into collage artwork where he blends a wide variety of source materials such as maps, picture book jackets, and magazines to often depict scenes of childhood. His work can be found in pediatric units of major hospitals across the country. A theme that often reoccurs in his work is that of hope and how we find it in every day with our relationship with others, whether they are our family or from far away distances and cultures.

Meet The Author ⟶

About the Author

Letta S. Baker Mason is a dedicated educator with a wealth of experience spanning from early childhood education to post-secondary institutions, including involvement in the juvenile justice system. Her career highlights include collaborating with President Mandela to implement the "Bridging the Gap Curriculum" and designing culturally responsive curricula for Princess Kasune Zulu of Zambia and S.T.E.M. programs for World Vision.

Letta has also worked alongside two Grammy artists as a songwriter and has authored four publications focused on Bringing the Arts to Life: Using Multiple Intelligences and Culturally Responsive Curriculum approaches to education. Letta is an A Early Childhood, Dual Language Adjunct Faculty at Evergreen State College Tacoma,, Child Development Instructor at Seattle Central College, Education Licensure Faculty at Goddard College, Plainsfield, Vermont, and Black Studies instructor and Curriculum Developer. As the owner of Sankofa Educational Services, Letta specializes in coaching teachers on implementing multiple intelligences and culturally responsive curriculum. Despite her professional accomplishments, Letta's most important role is nurturing her Scholars , grandScholars , and Scholars in the community who come into her life.

Made in the USA
Columbia, SC
05 August 2024

40a6804d-b1c7-4531-b045-94b1e4b3e664R01

BIBLIOGRAPHY

1. Pollock, A. S., Durward, B. R., Rowe, P. J. & Paul, J. P. What is balance? *Clin. Rehabil.* **14**, 402–406 (2000).

2. Shumway-Cook, A. & Woollacott, M. H. *Motor Control: Translating Research into Clinical Practice.* (Lippincott Williams & Wilkins, 2007).

3. Galica, A. M. *et al.* Subsensory vibrations to the feet reduce gait variability in elderly fallers. *Gait Posture* **30**, 383–7 (2009).

4. Amiridis, I. Age-induced modifications of static postural control in humans. *Neurosci. Lett.* **350**, 137–140 (2003).

5. Seidler, R. D. *et al.* Motor control and aging: links to age-related brain structural, functional, and biochemical effects. *Neurosci. Biobehav. Rev.* **34**, 721–33 (2010).

6. Shaffer, S. W. & Harrison, A. L. Aging of the somatosensory system: a translational perspective. *Phys. Ther.* **87**, 193–207 (2007).

7. Sturnieks, D. L., St George, R. & Lord, S. R. Balance disorders in the elderly. *Neurophysiol. Clin.* **38**, 467–78 (2008).

8. Michael, Y. L. *et al. Interventions to Prevent Falls in Older Adults: An Updated Systematic Review. Evidence Synthesis No. 80. AHRQ Publication No. 11-05150_EF-1.* (2010).

9. Lesinski, M., Hortobágyi, T., Muehlbauer, T., Gollhofer, A. & Granacher, U. Effects of Balance Training on Balance Performance in Healthy Older Adults: A Systematic Review and Meta-analysis. *Sport. Med.* **45**, 1721–1738 (2015).

10. Granacher, U., Zahner, L. & Gollhofer, A. Strength, power, and postural control in seniors: Considerations for functional adaptations and for fall prevention. *Eur. J. Sport Sci.* **8**, 325–340 (2008).

11. Gittings, N. S. & Fozard, J. L. Age related changes in visual acuity. *Exp. Gerontol.* **21**, 423–33 (1986).

12. Lord, S. R. & Dayhew, J. Visual risk factors for falls in older people. *J. Am. Geriatr. Soc.* **49**, 508–15 (2001).

13. Carpenter, M. G., Allum, J. H. & Honegger, F. Vestibular influences on human postural control in combinations of pitch and roll planes reveal differences in spatiotemporal processing. *Exp. Brain Res.* **140**, 95–111 (2001).

14. Horak, F., Nashner, L. & Diener, H. Postural strategies associated with somatosensory and vestibular loss. *Exp. Brain Res.* **129,** 167–177 (1990).

15. Magnusson, M., Enbom, H., Johansson, R. & Pyykkö, I. Significance of pressor input from the human feet in anterior-posterior postural control. The effect of hypothermia on vibration-induced body-sway. *Acta Otolaryngol.* **110**, 182–8 (1990).

16. Patel, M., Magnusson, M., Kristinsdottir, E. & Fransson, P.-A. The contribution of mechanoreceptive sensation on stability and adaptation in the young and elderly. *Eur. J. Appl. Physiol.* **105**, 167–73 (2009).

17. Kanekar, N. & Aruin, A. S. The effect of aging on anticipatory postural control. *Exp. Brain Res.* **232**, 1127–1136 (2014).

18. Buford, T. W., Anton, S. D., Clark, D. J., Higgins, T. J. & Cooke, M. B. Optimizing the Benefits of Exercise on Physical Function in Older Adults. *PM&R* **6**, 528–543 (2014).

19. Ng, C. A. C. M. *et al.* Exercise for falls prevention in community-dwelling older adults: Trial and participant characteristics, interventions and bias in clinical trials from a systematic review. *BMJ Open Sport Exerc. Med.* **5**, 1–10 (2019).

20. Sousa, N., Mendes, R., Silva, A. & Oliveira, J. Combined exercise is more effective than aerobic exercise in the improvement of fall risk factors: A randomized controlled trial in community-dwelling older men. *Clin. Rehabil.* **31**, 478–486 (2017).

21. Zaleski, A. L. *et al.* The FITT-V Principle of the ExR x Professional Committee/Organization ACSM/AHA 7,31 CDC 9 NIH 45 CSEP 46 BSG 47 WHO 48. 98–104 (2016).

22. Sherrington, C. *et al.* Exercise for preventing falls in older people living in the community: An abridged Cochrane systematic Review. *Br. J. Sports Med.* 1–8 (2019). doi:10.1136/bjsports-2019-101512

23. Granacher, U., Muehlbauer, T., Gollhofer, A., Kressig, R. W. & Zahner, L. An intergenerational approach in the promotion of balance and strength for fall prevention - a mini-review. *Gerontology* **57**, 304–15 (2011).

24. Granacher, U., Muehlbauer, T. & Gruber, M. A qualitative review of balance and strength performance in healthy older adults: Impact for testing and training. *J. Aging Res.* **2012**, (2012).

25. Granacher, U., Lacroix, A., Muehlbauer, T., Roettger, K. & Gollhofer, A. Effects of core instability strength training on trunk muscle strength, spinal mobility, dynamic balance and functional mobility in older adults. *Gerontology* **59**, 105–113 (2013).

26. Moran, J., Ramirez-Campillo, R. & Granacher, U. Effects of Jumping Exercise on Muscular Power in Older Adults: A Meta-Analysis. *Sports Medicine* **48**, 2843–2857 (2018).

27. Lomas-Vega, R., Obrero-Gaitán, E., Molina-Ortega, F. J. & Del-Pino-Casado, R. Tai Chi for Risk of Falls. A Meta-analysis. *J. Am. Geriatr. Soc.* **65**, 2037–2043 (2017).

28. Zhong, D. *et al.* Tai Chi for improving balance and reducing falls: An overview of 14 systematic reviews. *Annals of Physical and Rehabilitation Medicine* (2020). doi:10.1016/j.rehab.2019.12.008

29. Youkhana, S., Dean, C. M., Wolff, M., Sherrington, C. & Tiedemann, A. Yoga-based exercise improves balance and mobility in people aged 60 and over: A systematic review and meta-analysis. *Age Ageing* **45**, 21–29 (2016).

30. Varela-Vásquez, L. A., Minobes-Molina, E. & Jerez-Roig, J. Dual-task exercises in older adults: A structured review of current literature. *J. Frailty, Sarcopenia Falls* **05**, 31–37 (2020).

31. Brand, R. & Ekkekakis, P. Affective–Reflective Theory of physical inactivity and exercise: Foundations and preliminary evidence. *Ger. J. Exerc. Sport Res.* **48**, 48–58 (2018).

32. Antoniewicz, F. & Brand, R. Learning to like exercising: Evaluative conditioning changes automatic evaluations of exercising and influences subsequent exercising behavior. *J. Sport Exerc. Psychol.* **38**, 138–148 (2016).

33. Jekauc, D. & Brand, R. Editorial: How do Emotions and Feelings Regulate Physical Activity? *Front. Psychol.* **8**, 1145 (2017).

34. Wienke, B. & Jekauc, D. A Qualitative Analysis of Emotional Facilitators in Exercise. *Front. Psychol.* **7**, 1296 (2016).

35. Oettingen, G. & Gollwitzer, P. M. Strategies of Setting and Implementing Goals. In *Social Psychological foundations of Clinical Psychology* (eds. Maddux, J. & Tangney, J.) 114–135 (Guilford Press, 2010).

Printed in Great Britain
by Amazon